"Dowse (dowz, sometime dowss) intr. v ...
To use apparently paranormal senses
to make discoveries."
(17th century: origin obscure)

First published by Penwith Press 2002
This edition © Wooden Books Ltd 2009

Published by Wooden Books Ltd.
8A Market Place, Glastonbury, Somerset

British Library Cataloguing in Publication Data
Miller, H.
Dowsing, a journey beyond our five senses

A CIP catalogue record for this book is
available from the British Library

ISBN 1 904263 53 4

Printed and bound in Shanghai, China,
by Shangahi iPrinting Co., Ltd.

DOWSING

A JOURNEY BEYOND OUR FIVE SENSES

by

Hamish Miller

with illustrations by Jean Hands

Dedicated to Mortimer,
and all who are prepared to take responsibility for themselves
and enjoy their own free-will.

Unreferred pictures are 'Practica Minerale' by Marco Antonio della Fratta, 1678 (above), 'Report on Mines' by Georg Engelhard Löhneyss, 1617 (page 3t), 'Speculum Metallurgiae Politissimum' by Balthazar Rössler, 1700 (frontispiece and page 5t). For further reading contact the British Society of Dowsers, 2 St Ann's Rd, Malvern, Worcestershire, WR14 4RG, email: info@britishdowsers.org, who have a splendid library and addresses of dowsing groups all round the world.

Contents

INTRODUCTION

The delight about dowsing is that everybody can. Some better than others, but it usually depends on how much practice you put in. Like playing golf, a piano or making love you seem to get better the more you do it.

The old dictionary definition was uncompromising: "... the use of pendulum or rods to find water or minerals ...", but happily in recent years there has been a considerable break-through in the appreciation of dowsing ability. A more informed establishment recognising the increased scope and importance of the art has redefined it as "... the use of apparently paranormal powers to make discoveries".

So dowsing has undergone a paradigm shift from the useful but relatively mundane science of finding water sources, lumps of metal and old drains to the realms of a spiritual search into the mysteries of human consciousness and its relationship with the earth.

There is a practical, exciting journey waiting for everyone interested in the skill. It can lead by progressive expansion of thought to perceptions far beyond the normal restrictions of our five senses.

Better to start simply, learn the use of the various tools, find the one which suits you best, and grow slowly.

Penzance, April 2002

HISTORY
thousands of years of dowsing

In the mid 5th century BC the 'father of history' Herodotus the Greek reported the use of wooden Y-forks for the finding of water while he was roving around Scythia north of the Black Sea. It's the first written evidence of true dowsing, although there are references to similar functions in ancient Chinese literature.

Cave drawings from thousands of years ago have been claimed to depict dowsing implements of various shapes but it's difficult to believe that these slightly hairy outlines are anything to do with dowsing. A silver coin struck in 936 AD clearly shows a wee man with a forked stick in action above mine workings.

Martin Luther outrageously pronounced that it was "Devil's Work" in the early 16th century and as a result the art has been fiercely opposed by religious establishments for centuries. Fortunately the knowledge was preserved and passed on quietly by people who lives were closely connected to the earth.

About the same time a German mineralogist and metallurgist called Georgius Agricola published *De Re Metallica*, a treatise which included precise details of dowsing techniques in mining (*opposite top*). It aroused considerable interest in the industry throughout Europe although Agricola himself, still acutely conscious of the association of the art to the occult, hedged his bets by admonishing prospective miners "not to make use of the enchanted twig".

Miners using magical dowsing rods to discover hidden veins of ore

DEVELOPMENT
by royal command

Elizabeth I of England first got wind of the valuable 'forked stick' methods of finding metal ores through Agricola's work and introduced German miners to help develop England's resources. They brought their knowledge of dowsing with them, and by 1660 Charles II, recognising the importance of the art to the financial success of the mining industry, demanded to know everything about the operation of the '*Baguette Divinitoire*' ... splendid name for a dowsing rod.

In 1693 Pierre de Lorrain, Abbé de Vallemont caused consternation in religious circles and Paris society by publishing his *Occult Physics* which included detailed illustrations of dowsing techniques (*lower opposite*). It was promptly put on the prohibited list by the Inquisition, and he was probably one of the first authors to create a bestseller by having his book banned. His work triggered a vigorous pro-and-anti debate in the world of scientists and religious leaders, leading to a proliferation of scientific tests on the abilities of dowsers over the next century.

In museums round the world there are some fine examples of 17th and 18th century artwork, including silver drinking mugs, paintings and Meissen pottery, which figure little men with Y-rods akimbo looking for minerals. The burgeoning mining industry was a major contributor to the development of dowsing and the art thrived under the increasing pressure to find more and more mineral and water sources.

European dowsers hard at work, surveying a line of underground water or mineral faulting

| 1.ᵉ Manier.ᵉ de tenir la Baguette. | 2.ᵉ Manier.ᵉ de tenir la Baguette. | 3.ᵉ Manier.ᵉ de tenir la Baguette. | 4.ᵉ Manier.ᵉ de tenir la Baguette. |

PIONEERS
an emerging science

In eighteenth century France, Germany and Italy, the use of 'wands', 'sceptres', 'bobbing-sticks', 'rods', 'pendulums' and 'forks' by various 'twitchers', 'deusers', 'twiggers', 'dowsers', and 'water-witchers' to find all sorts of things became fair game for scientists and priests to investigate, and for the public to have fun with. A plethora of essays and publications by Lebrun, Menestrier, Zeidler, Albinus and Thouvenal fired broadsides at each other for and against the mysterious art.

Barthelemy Bleton, a brilliant natural water-witcher, working with the Bishop of Grenoble (author of the 'Bishop's Rule' for finding the depth of water) became the focus of Thouvenal's attempt to associate dowsing with electrical effects, but physicists could find no simple explanation of his talents.

Further work in Italy with the elegant Pennet, who constantly confounded observers by achieving remarkably accurate results (*shown aloft opposite*), still failed to persuade the authorities that dowsing was a talent worthy of serious debate. On the contrary it seemed that as 'absolute proof' in scientific terms was not readily available it was easier to accept the French astronomer Lalande's arrogant dismissal of all dowsing as trickery. He put dowsing rods in the same category as 'flying ships' declaring that "it is impossible for a man to raise himself from the ground". A year later the Montgolfier brothers were off in their first balloon.

PRACTITIONERS
excitement reborn

In the late eighteenth century William Cookworthy of Plymouth, England gave the art a shot in the arm by chronicling the undeniable talents of the Cornish mining dowsers. They had earned their reputation purely by the accurate results they had produced for that very tough industry, and had begun to be rewarded accordingly.

For a time local people who 'could just do it' were used to find water sources, but gradually some eminent Victorian British and Irish geologists became aware of the growing water needs of industry and the larger estates. One of the greatest practitioners of all time was Wiltshire's John Mullins. The legendary stories of his successes probably did more to make dowsing acceptable in the right circles than any contemporary academic papers.

In 1912 the mighty *Metallica* was translated from Latin to English by *Mining Magazine* in London, and sparked a fresh interest for many lateral thinkers of all disciplines. Then, in 1969, Guy Underwood's *The Patterns of the Past* broke new ground by exploring in meticulous detail the energies of sacred sites and their connections with water (*illustrations opposite*).

In 1976 Tom Lethbridge's *The Power of the Pendulum* explored other realities and in 1978 their work and the perceptions of John Michell inspired Tom Graves to write *Needles of Stone*, a dowsing book which introduced far-reaching concepts of our relationship with earth and cosmic energies.

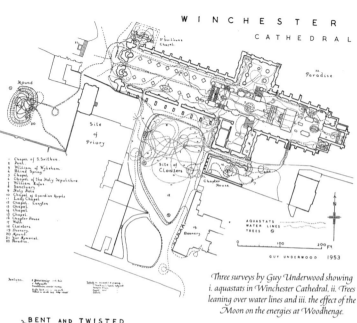

W I N C H E S T E R
C A T H E D R A L

St Swithuns
Chapel

Paradise

Mound

Site
of
Priory

Site
of
Cloisters

Chapter
House

1. Chapel of S.Swithun.
2. Font.
3. William of Wykeham.
4. Blind Spring.
5. Chapel.
6. Chapel of the Holy Sepulchre.
7. William Rufus.
8. Sanctuary.
9. Holy Hole.
10. Chapel of Guardian Angels.
11. Lady Chapel.
12. Chapel. Langton.
13. Chapel.
14. Chapel.
15. Chapter House.
16. Well.
17. Cloisters.
18. Deanery.
19. Deanery.
20. Mound.
21. War Memorial.
22. Paradise.

Deanery

AQUASTATS
WATER LINES
TREES

0   100   200 Ft.

GUY UNDERWOOD 1953

*Three surveys by Guy Underwood showing
i. aquastats in Winchester Cathedral. ii. Trees
leaning over water lines and iii. the effect of the
Moon on the energies at Woodhenge.*

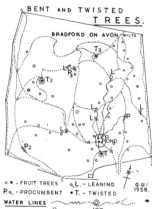

BENT AND TWISTED
T R E E S.

BRADFORD ON AVON. WILTS

T₃

T₂

POND

P₂

o ● - FRUIT TREES   L - LEANING
P - PROCUMBENT   T - TWISTED

G.U.
1958.

WATER LINES

0   100
Ft.

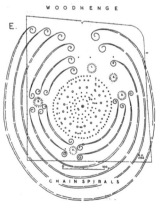

WOODHENGE

E.

C H A I N S P I R A L S

9

PROTAGONISTS
blazing the trail

In the last few decades an international array of dowsers have applied their talents to an expanding range of dowsing disciplines.

Terry Ross from Vermont could find water for villages in Mexico by instructing a surrogate dowser over the telephone, and wrote that dowsing could lead ultimately to "co-creation with nature". Bill Lewis of Wales had an awesome talent for finding objects in all parts of the world without leaving his home, and Roger Brown from Australia accurately recorded complex manifestations of earth energy field changes for a hundred-mile radius around Adelaide.

Russian specialists like Pluzhnikkov could pin-point mineral resources and archeological remains, and paranormal expert Neklessa developed a unique combination of pairs of scientists and mystics working together using advanced dowsing techniques to investigate the reasons for the failure of historic civilisations.

Many 'doodlebuggers' across the USA are fine-tuned to locate obscure oil deposits, while Elizabeth Sulivan of Wales is recognised by the authorities as an expert on the location of humans and animals by map dowsing. Colin Bloy in Spain initiated a sophisticated form of the dowsing process in the delicate art of healing, additionally applying it to the energy centres or 'haras' of towns and villages to improve the quality of life of people living there ... the list is endless and confirms a global interest in the art.

11

TOOLS
as long as they work

There are almost as many variations of tools as there are competent dowsers. Some are ingenious and some downright hilarious - a Californian one made from bent wire in the form of a continuous Greek Key pattern was five feet long and had to have a piece of broderie anglaise on the end.

It doesn't matter in the least, as long as it works. To work it has to be a comfortable link between the mind of the dowser and the target, the tool acting as an amplifier of the dowser's reactions.

Most people learn with one of three types, angle-rods, pendulums and Y-rods, but some prefer a form of 'bobber' or a wire loop. Y-rods were originally preferred because they could be conveniently cut from a hedge near the site where they were to be used, while bobbing sticks at this time were usually thin, sometimes shaped, slightly-curved branches. The Romans used pendulums, and rods developed later as metal became available.

Some practiced dowsers use their hands, with fingers moving in unison like a bunch of little L rods, or with their thumbs throbbing on forefingers. New materials such as carbon fibre have allowed dowsers to create imaginative, lightweight, sensitive and discreet tools to help them in their searches.

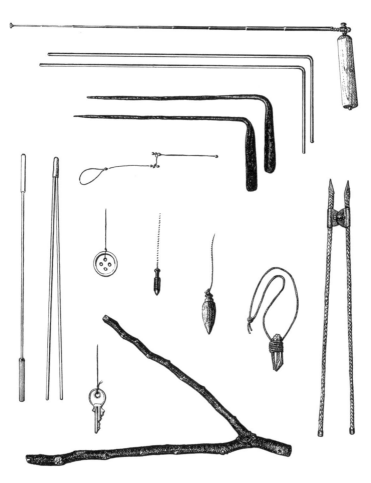

Choose your weapon: telescopic rod by Alan Heiss folds to pocket size and extends to 25";
Hand-forged bespoke rods in iron from Hamish; Guy Underwood's tricky wire loop device;
'Y' rods in discreet carbon fibre 8" long; Copper-hinged horse whips!

MAKING & HOLDING TOOLS
rods, pendulums and Y-rods

Rods can be bent from welding or brazing rod or chopped coat-hangers. Leave about 4-5 inches for the handle and crop wee bits off the long end until the balance feels good. Hold them level about fifteen inches apart in front of you in each hand like the Sundance Kid and relax.

Pendulums consist of something flexible tied to a weight. The 'cord' can be thread, string, chain, or plaited hair from your partner. You should have some rapport with the weight, like a favourite old ring, locket or miniature bottle of Lagavulin. Crystals are fine if you are careful but they sometimes have memories which can confuse your results.

Hold the cord about 6 inches above the weight at first to get used to its movement. It will start wobbling about even when your hand is still.

Y-rods can be cut from a willow or hazel in the shape of a fork, or split from a single branch, or made from carbon fibre or wire rods fixed together at one end. These have to be tensioned to work (*see opposite*). Bobbers can be whippy sticks or wires with springs and knobs, like the one below.

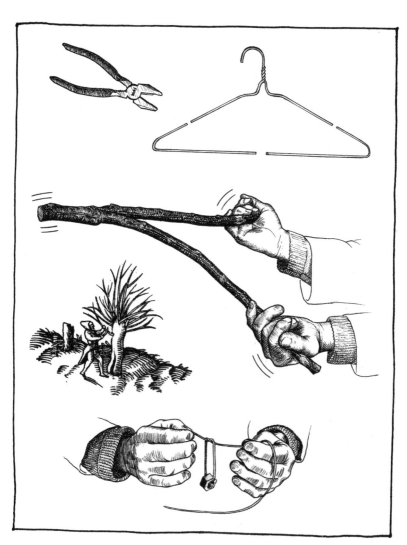

USING THE TOOLS
a simple start

The first essential is to establish a trustworthy *'yes'* or *'no'*.

Hold a pendulum in front of you with the cord between your thumb and forefinger, with the weight around six inches below your fingers. Swing it away from you and allow it to move freely. Concentrate and ask it firmly to show you a *'yes'*. In its own time it will change from a back and forward to a circular motion. Check to see if it is clockwise or counter-clockwise. Repeat the process for *'no'* and you'll find it revolves the other way. Practice this repeatedly until the pendulum becomes a natural extension of your hand. The tool sometimes changes its mind so check your *'yes'* every time before starting to dowse.

Using two rods, hold them in your hands about fifteen inches apart. They often cross for a *'yes'* and open out for *'no'*. Once they've decided, they don't usually mess about like pendulums.

A single rod gives a strong result. Hold it in front of you in your working hand, moving it slowly forward as you ask the question. If it turns the answer is *'yes'*, if nothing happens the answer is *'no'*.

Y-rods and bobbers do not respond for *'no'* and leap about for *'yes'*.

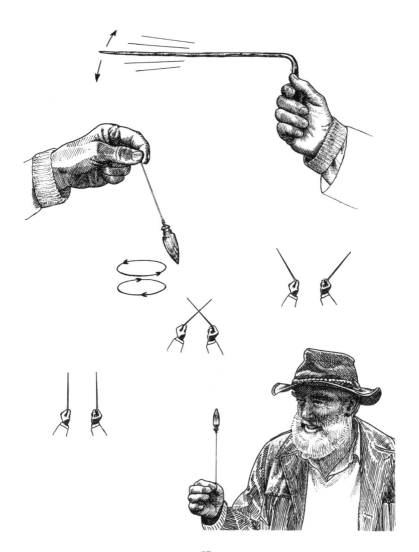

17

PRACTICE
next steps forward

Working on the hugely important *'yes'* and *'no'* will have given you a chance to judge your responses to the different tools. When you've decided which one you prefer, practice with questions like *where is the kitchen sink?*. The tool will soon get the idea and point in the right direction.

Try dowsing separate glasses with bottled water, tap water and red wine, asking if they are okay to drink. Now try it with water from the drain. Check the red wine to see if a few more would do you any harm. Dowse to see if the cheese you've left in the fridge is alright for you and your family to eat. If not would it be good for the cat? The answers will be *'yes'* or *'no'* but shouldn't be acted on until you have a lot of faith in your dowsing capability. Use your chosen weapon to find out if it's going to rain when you go shopping. Will everyone be happier if you do go and visit your mother-in-law? Should you just drop everything and go to Ibiza?

Above all practice your new talent, even though you do get wet between shops.

FIRST TRIALS
feeling the magic

Get used to handling your chosen tool. It's easier if you're not too ambitious or anxious at first. Work with it sitting, standing, walking, indoors, outside in the rain or under the bed until you are completely familiar with its movements.

Cheat a little to start with. Place a rope, cable or pipe on the grass or carpet and approach it with your eyes open, asking the tool to show you where it is. Now do it with eyes shut and preferably alone to avoid distractions. Get a friend to hide a bottle of your favourite wine in the garden, or a playing card under the carpet, and see if you can find it. Repeat, repeat, and repeat the exercise until your confidence grows.

It's all about tuning your mind. The aim is complete relaxation in body and thoughts but keeping one tiny part of your mind *totally* concentrated on the target. The dowsing tool provides a physical response to receptors in your consciousness which are capable of probing beyond normal sense horizons.

100% concentration makes you're right every time, very boring, and you can walk through walls, so a little humility helps.

Above all don't despair if you can't do it first time. It *is* only a matter of practice and if you really need a drink you'll find the bottle.

WITNESSES & QUESTIONS
helping to focus

The sole purpose of a *witness* is to assist in concentration. Any help to improve visualisation of the target is valuable and witnesses can be pieces of pipe, wire, metal, wood, or phials of water which can be conveniently held in your hand or attached to your person. Professor Henri Mager's witness is a circular disc about four inches in diameter which is divided into eight equal sections of various colours which help to discern different qualities in water. Rod dowsers use one rod while the other hand indicates the different colours of the witness. Y-fork people sometimes need six fingers.

There is no doubt that using a physical reminder of the target helps to keep the mind from wavering. It's difficult to lug a drainpipe about, but then they are easy to visualise.

An equally important discipline to learn is in phrasing the right questions. They have to be clearly defined, positive, and geared to receiving precise answers. Like working with a computer you get a reaction to your input, not a reasoned response. If the answer needs judgement of any kind the request isn't valid. Aim to narrow the field of search with each succeeding question until you nail the target.

It's disconcertingly easy to get answers to the question you *think* you've asked and be totally mislead. If your tank runs dry and you dowse for the distance to the nearest garage - make sure you ask for one that sells petrol.

Mortimer ready for anything

23

WATERPIPES & STREAMS
easy to check

You probably have a rough idea where your watermain is, so try an experiment: Walk slowly across the area with dowsing tool at the ready, fix your supply pipe firmly in your mind, ignore the curious stares of your neighbour and ask it to show you the position. No bells will ring but rods will turn, pendulums swing, and Y-rods move up or down as your hands cross the pipe. Mark the position and try it again a couple of feet nearer the house until you have a positive line of points.

One way to find the depth is to stand on the line you've just found, walk slowly away from it at right angles and ask the tool to move at a distance equal to the depth of the pipe. This is known as the 'Bishop's Rule'. Another way is to use your simple *'yes'* and *'no'* by 'bracketing'. Stand over the pipe and ask if it is between one and five feet down; if *'yes'*, ask if it's between one and three feet, and so on. Go into inches if you want to be really fussy.

Deal with underground streams in the same way. With your *'yes'* and *'no'* you can also find the width, direction of flow, flow rate, purity and whether you should add it to your whisky.

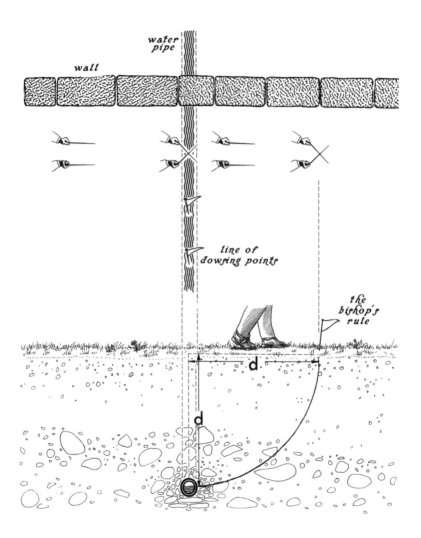

water
pipe

wall

line of
dowsing points

the
bishop's
rule

d

d

BUILDINGS & ARCHAEOLOGY
time savers

Huge amounts of time and money can be saved by the quick and accurate location of old foundations, sewage tanks, cables and drains. Archaeologists tend to have to take earth out by the thimbleful and a spot of dowsing can work wonders.

Directional dowsing is a useful start. Having decided exactly what you are looking for, find the direction of the target from where you stand by simply asking the tool to show you (just as you practiced with the kitchen sink). From a circular motion the pendulum will change to swinging in line with it. Rods will swivel to point at your objective from the site perimeter. Y-rods will dip or rise in the right direction as you turn around.

Move closer in the direction you've found and start defining your needs more clearly i.e "Show me a corner of the old wall, tank or Roman bath". With small objects ask the pendulum to whistle round, rods to cross, or bobbers bob directly over the medieval glass eye or priceless torque.

You can now use your '*yes*' or '*no*' bracketing technique to find out how old your treasure is and discover how deep you have to dig in the usual way.

1745   1820

MAP & CHART
another reality

The concept of dowsing from a map or chart seems to trigger disbelief. It is, however, perfectly logical, since the essence of dowsing is to find things which are normally hidden. The map or chart in itself is not important, but acts as a representation of the area of search which enables you to create a dowseable reality.

Once you are in there you can work in the ordinary way. One method is to triangulate from three points of the map so that you can pin a position with three directional lines. Or with a bobber, single rod or pendulum you can use the square grid system by slowly moving a finger along two sides of the map, asking if your target is in the row your finger is on. After you've done it both ways you end up with one small square.

Use a pencil to do the same operation in miniature. The larger the scale the more accurate you will be, so blow the guilty square up (on a photocopier, of course). Many a cell-phone and mudspattered rabbit-chasing terrier have been thankfully restored to their owners using these methods.

Specialist dowsers, who have to be very respectable, use maps to help the police find drugs, bodies and top secret laptops left in bars by MI5. American and British military dowsers have been involved, amongst other things, in underground tunnel, booby-trap, and mine detection.

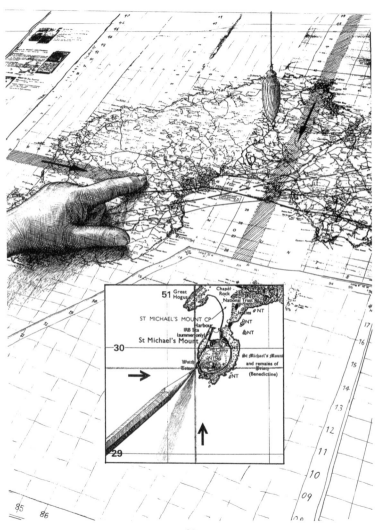

HEALTH & ALLERGIES
a handy tool

There is a growing awareness that health risks may be associated with the proliferation of chemically-sanitised processed foods, and dowsing can provide an interesting new level of interpretation as to whether our intake is beneficial or otherwise. It can also be a useful tool in the medical field to access information on allergies.

Use a pendulum, single rod or bobber, leaving the other hand free to move. The standard *'yes'* or *'no'* technique works well if you run your finger down a list of chemicals, medicines, foods, drinks, dusts, pollens, stings and so on, asking the tool to indicate whether the subject is allergic to any of them. It's a quick way of eliminating the harmless ones in what can otherwise be a time-consuming business. Probably more importantly you can find out what is *good* for you.

Fortunately Lagavulin comes very high on my positive list.

The rate of the swing of the pendulum, the speed and force with which the rods turn (I make flattened handles on my rods to give me a 'feel' of the movement), or the rapidity of the motion of the bobber can soon be recognised and assessed in a sort of personal Richter scale of one to ten. Some dowsers use calibrated scales to help analysis.

Using the same methods you can find out which potions have a healing effect, and whether it's okay to have another dram.

BODY ENERGIES & CHAKRAS
an extra dimension

Our bodies don't end at the surface of the skin; we are surrounded by assorted energy fields which some people can sense but few of us discern with our five senses.

The *aura* is very basic and we have a number of other main biomagnetic fields called *chakras* which we share with every animal, insect, plant, stone and mini-piece of matter in the universe. Through them we are connected to everything on earth and finally to the cosmos.

Dowsing is a way of perceiving these fields as a reality. Use a pendulum, bobber or rod to show you where the aura starts. It will register at a point around twelve to thirty inches away from the body depending on the health of the volunteer and where he or she is standing, and as you follow the contour round it will show how the bio-field varies in depth in certain places.

If it's depleted at any point it could indicate that there is a potential problem in the area or that a physical defect is already there. Luckily you can help revitalise the aura and chakras by directing energy at them using your fingers like a pistol.

Some of the chakras are very subtle and it's easier to dowse them with your hands. You'll probably get a slight tingling or a feeling of resistance like a soft balloon.

33

CHURCHES
discretion is the better part

Many, if not most, ancient churches are built on sacred sites which were used as meeting places for social, ritual and spiritual events long before the Christian era. Succeeding religious authorities recognised the power of these places and, by superimposing their structures on them, sought to preserve the energy while establishing the new dogma. Earth energy is cosmopolitan and reacts to genuine prayer and ritual irrespective of which deity inspires it.

Unfortunately there is no simple structure to energy patterns in churches now; through the ages eager clergy, anxious sinners and their builders have moved fonts and altars, and arranged for endless alterations of the present buildings with little understanding of the earth-energy balances which provide the ambience of sanctity, peace and purity.

It often happens, with a good vicar and a congregation who attend for the right reasons, that the main power centre of the church stays firmly in position on the centre-line of the building, and about six inches in from the front of the altar. These are the churches which feel welcoming when you enter and it's interesting to check the energy centre in the usual way, using discretion in the use of dowsing tools.

Many of the priesthood are very much aware of the energy fields and their effects. In fact quite a number are dowsers, but it's always better to have a quiet word first to avoid offence.

35

CATHEDRALS
sacred knowledge

A staggering number of Gothic cathedrals were built in twelfth century Europe under the guidance and support of the Knights Templar. Their aim was to use their newly acquired knowledge of telluric currents (earth energies), resonance, sacred geometry, space, and colour to create stone monuments which would inspire mankind to reach ever higher levels of spiritual development.

They were acutely aware that the etheric human senses are profoundly affected by underground caves and dolmen, and often chose to place their new structures on these recognised and established power points.

The choice of site was delicate and deliberate, making the best use of the earth's pure energy, one of its greatest but least understood gifts to us. The caves became crypts below buildings constructed by trained master craftsmen who used stressed stone and sound in geometric harmony to create the numinous balance of vibration and resonance.

For budding dowsers there is no more awesome place to practice earth energy work than around a cathedral. As the complexities begin to unravel it's possible to glimpse some of the sophistication of the knowledge behind the space, structure and its relationship with the earth.

Cuts us down to size a bit.

DOWSING THE EARTH'S FIELD
free connection

There is an inconceivably vast and complex network out there which makes our primitive internet look neanderthal. Each one of us is already linked in, and while for a time we lost the delicate art of tuning in to the whispering energies of the universe, dowsing has re-opened a door for us to return to our evolutionary birthright.

Every field, garden and house has its own energy centres and you can locate the most powerful one in the same way as you found the kitchen sink. Work with it consciously and ask if you may communicate with it. It will respond to the right approach by manifesting energy lines like the spokes of a wheel in straight lines from the centre.

Walk slowly round the point asking the tool to show you where the lines are. Mark them on the carpet or grass. Usually they are bunched closer together in one or two directions and it's likely that other earth energy connections come in at these points.

Walk in towards the centre on each radial (not necessarily in sequence) and ask to be shown where any other manifestation crosses the line.

When you've located and marked them all you'll find a perfect Fibonacci spiral winding out from the centre. This is one of the basic building blocks of the universe and is so awesome that your hair will probably stand on end.

LEY & ENERGY LINES
the earth is listening

A *ley line* is a straight alignment of at least four significant or sacred sites. They were named by Alfred Watkins who was the first man to notice that there were lots of them all over the countryside (*opposite top*). While volumes have been written about the significance of these line-ups the main interest for dowsers is with the energy flows which weave around the lines and pulse in the sacred sites. It's almost as though the ley lines are there as pointers to places of power. The old people, who knew a thing or two about power points, went to enormous lengths moving great stones around the countryside to mark them with sophisticated geometrical structures.

Every energy line is made up from a marginally different set of frequencies giving each a 'signature' which can, with practice, be identified by a dowser as easily as a favourite label on a shelf. They are the earths' equivalent of our nervous and meridian systems and throb to the rhythms of the universe.

Undulating across the countryside in pairs, one polarity tends to hug the higher ranges and hilltops while the other seeks out valleys, plains and water. The combined energies of their sporadic meetings create spiritually uplifting backwaters of balanced purity which have a profound effect on the bio-magnetic fields around our bodies. For ages Far Eastern cultures have been aware of the importance of these delicate energies and have developed sophisticated expertise in their use in *feng shui*.

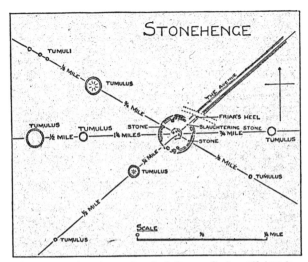

Above: Leys around Stonehenge, as drawn by the discoverer of ley lines, Alfred Watkins.
Below: The 'Michael Line' of ancient sacred sites across the south of England, with its two currents.

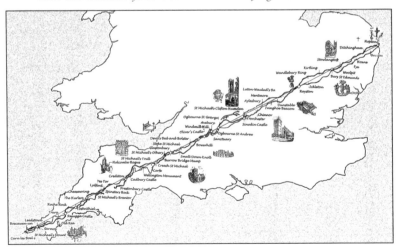

41

SACRED SITES
centres of power

Sacred sites and energy lines must have been of paramount importance to the ancients. It requires a disciplined society with unwavering convictions through generations to create monuments like Avebury and Stonehenge in Wiltshire, England. Even the lesser stone circles scattered around country required monumental effort to create, and we are fortunate that the old ones chose this method of permanent marking.

Dowsing a stone circle to access its energy field is a rewarding exercise. There are often eight energy lines round the perimeter which seem to act as 'sensors', switching on the field for any consciousness willing to tune in. Find the power centre (not necessarily the geometric centre) in the usual way and from that point pick up the energy spiral. A number of lines radiate like irregular spokes of a wheel from the centre, each one passing through a stone. Each stone is connected to all the others, every one has its own spiral and radials, and the resulting field is a complex, vibrant energetic web (*lower right opposite*). Take time to dowse the separate magnetic fields of each stone and carefully phrase the questions you are prompted to ask.

One of the most powerful sites in the U.K. is on St Michael's Mount in Cornwall where two pairs of strong global earth energy lines meet in perfect harmony creating a vortex of peaceful stimulating space where cosmic energies connect with the earth's field. No spin doctors on this network.

St. Michael's Mount, Cornwall, where two pairs of global energy lines cross. The Michael and Mary lines run NE-SW, whereas the other pair hop over to Mont St. Michel, Bourges and Cluny in France, on through Sacra di San Michele, Pisa, Siena, Assisi and Promontaro Gargano in Italy, then through Delphi and Athens in Greece (where they go by the names of Apollo and Athena) and finally off to Mount Carmel and the Holy Land.

crossing energy lines, St. Michael's Mount, and the Merry Maidens Stone Circle, Cornwall

SACRED EARTH
global links

All over the world there are sacred sites which have long been connected with stories handed down through generations of indigenous people. These mythical folk-memories are an amalgam of occult knowledge and profound spiritual awareness, and they have so many factors in common world-wide that some form of prehistoric communication between sites must have existed.

Ethnic groups from Texas to Tashkent, from the Kalihari to Kabul and from the Chilean Andes to China each developed a special reverence for their local sites, and their legends show that while there are some differences in their interpretation of events and manifestations, there are positive connections between them which are contrary to accepted historical record.

Possible global earth-energy linkage structures have been suggested by Berenholtz of Los Angeles, Coon of Glastonbury and other international writers and thinkers. The energies of sites like Mt. Shasta (*opposite top*), Machu Pichu, and Uluhuru are as varied as the cultures which previously understood them, and as more and more people tune in to their frequencies, the old links between these sacred places are expanding and increasing in strength.

Dowsers are taking the opportunities now available to visit and assess similarities and variations of energy manifestations at these glorious, stimulating planetary acupuncture points, and are finding that exposure to the powerful energies is a richly rewarding experience. It's a lot more exciting than lying on the beach.

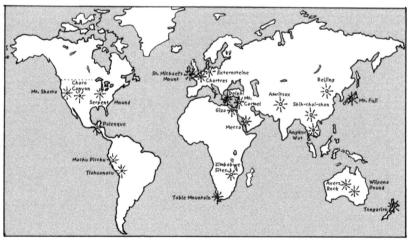

EARTH'S ENERGY FIELD
cosmic internet

Druid legend has it that there are twelve main lines of energy round the world, not necessarily great circles, but joining and feeding the great power centres of the planet. These pathways are the equivalent of our spinal cord but earth has twelve because she's big and round.

The crossing places are very special and pulse with vortices of energy which connect with the universe. They are the gateways where peripatetic beings can come through into our density to learn and perhaps guide how we behave.

Joining these pathways are lesser energy lines which split, divide and subdivide endlessly, covering the globe on, under and above the surface until they are small enough to contact the energy centres of the minutest creatures and basic elements of the planet.

There is a growing interest amongst lateral thinking scientists and mathematicians in the perception and investigation of these natural fields and their effects on our biologicaldevelopment, particularly in the light of recent work on the measurable effects of sunspot activity on the earth's magnetic field.

The concept of being at one with the universe is easier to accept with this vision in our thoughts, and dowsing for it's reality can make an important contribution to the expansion of our minds.

It's a lot of fun, too.

EARTH ENERGY RESPONSES
the common language

A direct response between the earth and human consciousness seems impossible because of the language barrier between two such different beings. We have enough trouble communicating with dolphins who have to drop to their baby-talk to get down to our level. The earth, however, seems to be looking for solutions by responding to stimuli and manifesting geometric symbols at power centres in her energy field.

This response alone is awesome, almost beyond belief, but dowsing has shown that the recently discovered spiral shape pulses with the rhythms of the earth, the cyclic movements of moon, planets, sun, the state of our minds and doubtless many other factors of which at the moment we are unaware. Experiments have continued with ancient and modern artifacts placed on the energy centres and while by no means all of them stimulate a dowseable response, many of them activate a positive if sometimes asymmetric mathematical shape. We have found that natural energy forms can be profoundly affected by prayer and meditation and that the extent of any changes in the field pattern seems to be in direct proportion to the degree of mind concentration applied.

Not enough work has been done to come to any form of conclusion but this is an exciting new field for dowsers to work on, perhaps in conjunction with specialists in geology, resonance and magnetic fields.

Etruscan Pot 2000 BC

Convergence Sculpture 1997

Celtic God Medallion 1500 BC

Ancient Amber from Himalayas

Artifacts placed at energy centers produce individual dowseable shapes.

BEYOND TOOLS
our sensitive hands

There is a mystical excitement when first feeling dowsing tools move of their own accord, but none can touch, feel, manipulate and create as delicately as our own human hands. These can be programmed in the dowsing mode to a sense of awareness extending far beyond the skin. Learning to detect the body's ethereal boundaries with hands is a wonderful experience which profoundly changes our relationship with all of creation. However, it is of the greatest importance not to intrude on people, animals, plants or landscape when dowsing, and permission should always be obtained from whoever before starting.

Try pressing thumb and forefinger lightly together and becoming aware of changes of 'feel' as you work. Eventually you will find you are able to sense things without the response from your hands. Many people progress to a point where they see energy as coloured lines of light and some can apparently move into whatever environment they are researching. Dowse with rods or pendulums to identify shapes and images drawn by a friend, and you will gradually develop a form of telepathic communication which works without tools.

'Deviceless' dowsing can be used to mentally lock on to a water course and follow its meanderings, and is useful for work in sensitive areas where the obvious use of tools might cause offence. It can help discern sources of geopathic or social stress, or locate lost people, animals, car keys and dematerialised pairs of glasses.

TIME
a way to move through

There is no reason why our minds should be trapped in our earthly perception of time. The concept of dowsing out of present time is perfectly valid, but it needs a very special mental discipline to be sure of correct answers. Start by bracket-dowsing to find the age of grandmother's antique cameo pendant, check its age with an expert in the jewellery field, and use it to tune into the period. Once you've done that you can dowse normally holding the cameo in your hand as a witness, but of course you will have to train your mind to prevent an inadvertent return to 'now'.

Practice 'age'-dowsing on an newly-felled tree trunk. Have it checked by a dendrochronologist. If you have difficulty in saying it or finding one, count the annular growth rings yourself.

There are many talented experts in psychometry. This is an ability to access facts about objects, events and people by handling artifacts and tuning in to their past. It's a form of dowsing and works remarkably well when you have learned to prevent your rational mind from interfering.

Future events open a different can of worms. This is divination rather than dowsing and the confusion of the two terms triggered quite some opposition from the Church based on their interpretation of Deuteronomy 18;10. In my opinion it can't work because I believe that the future holds an infinite number of possibilities.

Not many dowsers win the lottery.

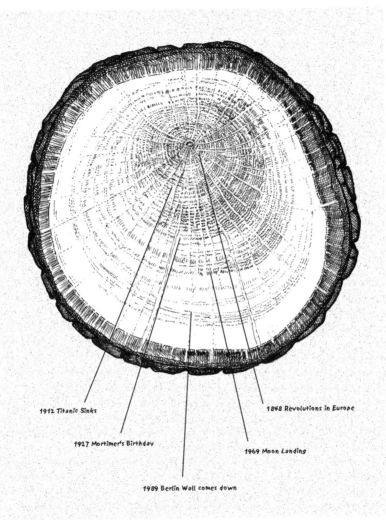

1912 Titanic Sinks

1927 Mortimer's Birthday

1989 Berlin Wall comes down

1848 Revolutions in Europe

1969 Moon Landing

REMOTE VIEWING
through the curtain

Dowsing deals with perceptions of events and objects which are normally hidden. *Remote viewing* is a highly specialised version of the art where the viewer develops an ability to tune, with a high degree of concentration, to specific targets anywhere in the world and beyond. Restrictions of time and travel no longer apply and experts can 'see' locations, situations and actions as they are happening. Accurate viewing requires a considerable mental discipline but this can gradually be acquired with practice by honing standard dowsing techniques. The trick is to transfer the complex energies which normally cause the rod or pendulum to move in a simple 'yes' or 'no', into the creation of a mental picture of the event.

Unfortunately some of the more advanced talents in this exciting field have been persuaded by military and political 'experts' to spend a lot of time in embassies trying to find out what the chaps next door are doing, and this tends to restrict the natural development of the skill. When we get beyond this archaic, sometimes paranoid, application of this wonderful human talent and more of us become proficient viewers, we may all have to think about becoming more honest. Difficult to cheat in business or run a war if the other side knows what you're up to.

This major dowsing breakthrough could one day help man's evolutionary progress simply by forcing us to be more open with each other.

BEYOND THE VEIL
quo vadis

While working on Earth's energies with her myriads of frequencies, you may occasionally come across a few which are not in resonance with the place or person. All natural earth energy is benign but sometimes it has been influenced by a less than pleasant human consciousness, and as a result of this can generate feelings of discomfort or even fear. Practiced dowsers can ask for these to be changed to healing frequencies in a way that does not affect any other being. There are many ritualistic ways of doing this with crystals, stones, metal pipes and even burning effigies, but if you are coming from the right place, all you have to do is ask. The effect can be extraordinarily beneficial and the process is very simple.

In dowsing we have a tool which stimulates senses beyond the usual five. It is one way of letting us recognise the limitations of our present perceptions. With the realisation that the social, spiritual, and moral restrictions which have historically controlled our thought patterns can be questioned, modified or lifted comes the freedom to make our own decisions about the life-style we would like to follow. Each of us needs the courage to accept the responsibility for the results of our decisions.

We can *all* do it if we work together with love, care and concern for the earth in all its manifestations.